Who are God's Children?

This book is written to correct an understanding that has plague Christians for generations.

Believers must pray for knowledge to understand all the difference voices we hear.

We must be able to separate those that God call to deliver his message from the ones that want to be seen.

© copyright 2015 Ralph L. Watts
All rights reserved
ISBN 978-0-9858029-8-1

This book is dedicated to
My Mother
Rosia Mae Gandy

And Daughters
Deborah D. Gates
Donna D. Wilkerson
Dayatra D. Arnold
D'Shawn D. Watts

And Special Nephew
Reverend Jimmy Hawkins
and wife
Reverend Joyce Hawkins
Special Niece
Mary Ann Daniels

May God Bless
You All

Author's Testimony

I have always loved, respected and recognized the important of human life. This affection kept a responsive mood; enticing the betterments of my life to love, honor and obey the righteousness.

Righteousness was my phenomenon. I believe if one was wrong, he could be shown and understand without detesting. I was wrong. The remission of an offense is exercised by the believers of God's faith.

God's faith makes righteousness a reality. Righteousness needs spiritual guidance to merit his words and action. This I found to be true.

Righteousness alone cannot guide man or his country. They must bond to a foundation of God's trust. This eliminates the oppression of many people.

God does not have commitments to any country that has oppressed people. It's unsafe and subject to destruction unless they recognize, cease and remission the true agony that is occurring...

Many of us mean well and want to be creative for our country. Without living the way intended (love one another) SUBSISTENCE IS NOT GUARANTEED.

Who Are God's Children is written for that purpose. It is written to define and understand the true meaning of our purpose on this earth.

<u>Author</u>

Chapters

I. In the Beginning   1

II. Noah   7

III. Noah's Children   9

IV. Abraham & Keturah   25

V. Abraham & Hagar   27

VI. Abraham & Sarah   29

VII. Jacob   31

VIII. The Israelites   40

IX. David	44
X. Solomon	48
XI. Jesus Christ	49
XII. Who Are God's Children?	50
XIII. What is borne again?	59
XIV. Racism in the Bible	74
XV. How should we live?	84
XVI. . Noted Bible Women	101
XVII. Absolute	106

Chapter I

In the Beginning

A good start would be from the beginning. As we all know in the beginning God created the heavens and the earth. Then he created man and woman.

In this creation he stated and created a female for a male. God did not make Adam a man or a woman for Eve. If we do anything other than what he created us for is ungodly. I think we got that straight.

I say this now to not having to interpret this action later.

He told them to go out and multiply after sin in the garden. This multiplication took many paths. Many of these paths were sinful and this created feelings that God resented.

Many scholars will say God knew in advance what man was going to do. How can man interpret what the almighty was thinking? He cannot match the mind of the almighty God. A matter of facts his way of thinking is the reason we are in this sinful world.

If man would have listen to his maker the world would be a wonderful place to live. All rules and laws produced would be accepted by God.

2

After Cain slew Abel sin began to multiply. The men and women lived an ungodly life very displeasing to God.

The wickedness of men became very great upon the earth. As far as the eyes could see and the mind could imagine sin was doubling every day.

As we seem to not understand sin was everywhere. In their homes, schools, churches, workplace and even in our Courts.

We as a people have decided in our life to accept this sin if it does not hurt you. All sins affect everybody one way or another. Just because it's not hurting today; tomorrow it will get you around the corner.

3

Where can you go where there is no sin? Is it at the grocery store or maybe the church? Speaking about a church let me tell about my experience of one church I loved to attend.

This church is a medium size with which I suppose are great people. This particular Sunday I got there a little late. So I had to accept a seat near the rear of the church. I took my seat and ready to enjoy the remaining service.

I happen to look to my right and this young lady was sitting there wearing a short and I mean short dress. I suppose she thought she was at a nightclub. Her dress was showing more than half of her thigh. I had to get up and leave. I will not let Satan intimidate me this way.

4

I went outside to my car and decided to wait until church out to see if there were others dress this way. Sure enough there were two others with their nightclub attire.

I said to myself do these ladies know the church suppose to be holy grounds? Do ministers teach members how to dress? Maybe I take things too seriously and should look the other way.

Is this what God expect of his children? Does looking the other way provide comfort to your soul?

We have many cases where we look the other way because its family, a friend or a friend's child. Sometimes we look the other way because that person is my nationality. Never-the-less looking the other way looses your place in God's Kingdom.

5

God's Kingdom is for God's children. That is what this book is about. Who are God's children will be explain in later chapters.

6

Chapter II

Noah

Geneses 6:1 tell us it came to pass, when men began to multiply on the face of the earth, and daughters were born unto them.

As they multiply so did sin. Geneses 6:5 tell us; and God saw the wickedness of man was great in the earth, and that every imagination of the thoughts of the heart was only evil continually.

God was dissatisfied with what Man had become. And he said I will destroy man whom I have created from the face of the earth.

The earth was corrupt and filled with violence. This is in our world today.

7

Noah was a God fearing man. He also found grace in the eyed of God.
God used Noah to build an ark to spare what is believed to be the only living godly souls.

Noah and his family were saved from destruction.

His three sons Japheth, Ham and Shem were to produce seventy (70) nations. Ham was assigned thirty (30) nations, Shem twenty-six (26) nations and Japheth fourteen (14) nations.

To the smart scholar: Why was Ham given thirty (30) nations?

Why was Japheth given only fourteen (14) nations?

8

Chapter III

Noah's Children

Shem
Had four sons

He lived about 600 years
His family was known as Semites

1. Elem (Elam)
Shem first son
The Elamites was once in the South western part of Iran.

Darius the Great came and took over and called himself a Persian. The Persians which is an Aryan seed came from Japheth seed.

9

The western world claims that Elam was not Shemitic even thou he is the son of Shem. The Elamites shared a link in the release of Israel from exile.

2. Asshur
Shem second son

Assyrians

The Assyrians worship a false god. They always carried the false god with them in battle. Also known as the father of Tekoa

Hepher
Asshur's first son

Temeni
Asshur's second son by Asshur second wife Naarah.

.

3. Arphaxed-Arpachshad
Shem third son

1. Salah-Sala
Arphaxed first son
Lived for 433 years

Eber
Shelah's son
Lived 192 years

11

Peleg
Eber's first son

Reu
Peleg son
Lived 240 years

Serug
Reu son Lived 229 years

Nahor
Serug son
Lived 149 years

Terah
Nahor son.
Father of Nahor, Abram and Haran
Lived 205 years

Nahor
Married Mileah the daughter of his brother Haran.

Abraham
Terah son
Father of a multitude
Lived for 175 years

Isaac
Abraham & Sarah son
Lived for 180 years

,

2. Joktan-
Eber second son
Arabia

13

1. Almodad
Joktan first son
Father of Ishmael wife

2. Sheleph
(Possible Yemen)
Joktan second son

3. Hazarmaveth
Joktan third son

4. Jerah
Joktan fourth son

5. Hadoram
Joktan fifth son
Yemen

14

6. Uzal
Joktan sixth son

7. Diklah
Joktan seventh son
Yemen

8. Obal
Joktan eighth son

9. Abimael
Joktan ninth son

10. Sheba
Joktan tenth son

15

11. Ophir
Joktan eleventh son

12. Havilah
Joktan twelfth son

13. Jobab
Joktan thirteenth son

4. Lud
Shem fourth son
Lydians
Asia

16

5. Aram (Syrians)
Shem fifth son
Aramaeans

1. Uz

2. Hul

3. Gether

4. Mash

They were known as nomads. They lived on the West side of the Syrian Desert. Sons are UZ, Hul, Gether & Mash (Aramaeans & Syrians)

17

This is the blood line of Jesus Christ
26 nations

Genealogical line from Shem to Abraham and to Jesus

Ham

All these nations are dislike by the west.

God granted Ham thirty Nations

18

Ham Children
30 nations

Cush-(Africa)
Seba,
Havilah,
Sabtah,-Arabia
Raamah,
Sabtechah,-Arabia

Nimrod-A mighty Hunter

Raamah sons=Sheba & Dedan

19

Mizraim-Egyptian Tribes
Sons

Ludim,

Anamim,

Lehabim

Pathrusim,

Casluhim & Caphtorim

Sidon-1st born
Heth

Jebusites lost, Amorites, Girgashites,
Hivites, Arkites, Sinites, Arvadites, Zemarites,
Hamathites, Hittites, Canaanites, Perizzites

20

Phut-Libyans

Canaan (Palestine, Egypt & Syria)-
Sidon (Zidon)
Heth&
Arkite &
Arvaditem &
Girgashites

Ethiopians, Egyptians, African tribes, Canaanites & some Arabian.

Progenitor of eleven (11) Tribes

Mizraim & Phut is northern Libyans

21

Hamitic peoples
Rahab
Boaz

Obed father of Jessie who was the father of David

Jezebel wife of Ahab (Dan 7:9 & Rev 1:14-15

22

Japheth Children

Japhetic world power of Medo-Persia, Greece & Rome

01. Gomer (Aryan)
  A. Ashkenaz
  B. Riphath
  C. Togarmah (Among Gog of Magog)
02. Magog
03. Madai
04. Javan
  A-Elishah
  B-Tarshech (Spain)
  C-Kittim (Italy)
  D-Dodanim

23

Dodanim (Rodanim). Greeks (Slave trader)

There is a price to pay for slave traders. As you see Japheth bloodline played an important part in harassing nations of color.

05.   Tubal
-Slave trader along with Meshech

06, Meshech
Slave trader along with Tubal

07. Tiras

14 Nations
Aryan or Indo-European, German, Europe and probably China

24

Chapter IV

Abraham and Keturah

Abraham sons by Keturah

First son- Zimrain

Second son- Jokshan,=
Sheba &
Dedan.
A. Assurim,
B. Letushim &
C. Leummim

Third son - Medan, (Arabian Tribe)

25

Fourth son- Midian=
Ephah,
Epher,
Hanoch,
Abidah &
Eldaah.

Fifth son- Ishbak

Sixth son- Shuah

All offspring's of Abraham and Keturah settled
In SE part of Palestine

26

Chapter V

Abraham & Hagar

Ishmael sons

Nebaioth

Kedar

Adbeel

Mibsam

Mishma

27

Dumah

Massa

Hadat

Tema

Jetur

Naphish

Kedeman

Mabalath-Daughter
Married Esau
The Ishmalites were about 1/3
Semitic & 2/3 Hamitic

28

Chapter VI

Abraham and Sarah

Isaac & Jacob

Isaac and Rebekah

Esau

Jeush

Jaalam

Reuel

Korah

29

Eliphaz

A. Teman

B. Omar

C. Zepho

D. Gatam

E. Kenaz

Chapter VII

Jacob

Jacob's Children

01. Reuben-
Oldest was by Leah #1=Reubenites (committed fornication with Bilhah after Rachel died).

Hanoch

Pallu

Hezron

Carmi

31

02. Simeon- #2 by Leah #2=Simeons
Jemuel
Jamin
Ohad
Jachin
Zohar
Shaul

03. Levi- #3 by Leah #3=Levites
Gershom
Kohath
Merari

04. Judah- # 4 by Leah #4=
Er
Onan
Shelah
Pharez
Zarah

32

05. Dan- #5 by Bilhah=Hushim (Samson)
Rachel maid=
Hushim-Shuham
A. Samson

Samson A skin colored Judge who was given a hard time among his people. The color of his skin made him a subject to all kinds of bad treatments.

06. Naphtali-#6 by Bilhah #2= Rachel
maid=
Jahzeel,
Guni,
Jezer &
Shiliem

07. Gad- #7 by Zilpah (Leah's maid) =

33

07. Gad- #7 by Zilpah (Leah's maid) =When the promise lane was divided; Gad who had the second largest family was given the smallest amount of land. This is so sad because everyone in the East know that was discriminatory. This cause other tribes and people in the East to dislike the light skin Isrealites because they were prejudice.

Ziphion,

Haggi,

Shuni,

Eri,

Ezbon,

Aroid (Arod, Arodi) & Areli

34

08. Asher- #8 by Zilpah #2=
Sons=
Jimnah,

Ishuah,

Isui,

Beriah,

A. Heber-Asher's grandson

B. Malchiel

Serah (daughter)

09. Issachar-#9 by Leah #5=
Tola

Puah

Jashub

Shimrom

35

10. Zebulun- #10 by Leah #6=
Sered
Alon
Jahleel

11. Joseph- #12 by Rachel #2=????#11
(XXX)
Manasseh &
Ephraim by Asenath

12. Benjamin- #11 by Rachel #1=????#12
(XXX)
1. Bela-Benjamin's first son

A. Ard=Benjamin's grandson

B. Gera

Huppaom-

Shephuphan

36

Naaman
2, Becher-Benjamin's second son

Ashbel or Jediael
\
4. Nohah
Rapha

6. Ahiram & Aharah & Ehi

Dinah-Daughter

Jacob on his death bed appointed Ephraim and Manasseh to be the equals of his direct sons.(Gen 48:5)

After the death of Solomon the Kingdom was divided. Ten tribes foaming the Northern Kingdom, called <u>Israel.</u> Two tribes which foamed the Southern Kingdom were called <u>Judah.</u> Judah and Benjamin formed the Southern Kingdom.

<u>The Northern Kingdom lasted for 200 years and destroyed by Assyria.</u>

<u>The Southern Kingdom lasted over 300 years and was destroyed by Babylon.</u>

Jeroboam founder of the Northern Kingdom worship the <u>Golden Calf.</u>
<u>Mostly all the 19 kings of Israel were very bad.</u>

Out of the 18 Kings of Judah, seven were very good. Asa, Jehoshaphat, Athaliah, Joash, Amaziah, Uzziah and Jotham

Bilhah
A Canaanite woman
Dan children
Hushim (?),
Naphtali,

38

Guni,

Jezer

Shillem

Zilpah

Gad Children

Ziphion,

Haggi,

Shuni,

Ezbon,

Eri,

Arodi

Areli.

39

Chapter VIII

The Israelites

The Israelites are the descendants of the twelve sons of Jacob.

Hosea 1:10 say the children of Israel shall be as the sand of the sea, Which cannot be measured nor numbered, and it shall come to pass, that in the place where it was said unto them, you are not my people, there it shall be said unto them, you are the sons of the living God.

Now I know people of the west will try to tell a different story. They will say this means that and this means this. But let the Bible speak! Where is there a nation like the sand of the sea? God is speaking about the people of Israel. Where are these people?

40

He is speaking about his twelve designated sons. Who are the sons? They are Reuben, Simeon, Levi, Judah, **Dan, Naphtali, Gad, Asher**, Issachar, Zebulun, Benjamin and Joseph.

There was trouble from the start. Discrimination played a part in every decision made among these tribes. Dan, Naphtali, Gad and Asher were always on the last in decision making.

This is nothing new. Remember Noah's children? Ham and Sham got along well because they had color skin but Japheth with was fair could not fit in.

41

Remember Governor Pilate in the year 33.

<u>The Jewish nation wanted Jesus crucified.</u>

Oh! How we forget the ugly things that happen. The question now; How can I love the man my nation is accused helping to crucify?

Did Jesus skin color have anything to do with the crucifixion?

One thing for sure we must be careful of what we speak and do.
Jesus hair was like lamb wool and feet of burnt brass. Do I have to say more? People that lives in the East know the West try to change the color of characters in the bible to make them look like westerners.

42

We must ask God for guidance so we make no mistake.

Remember Hosea 1:10; It said "you are not my people, there it shall be said unto them, you are the son of the living God".

Many nations have been labeled as one without God knowledge.

Only the Israelites understand who and what about Jesus salvation. Now they realize Jesus was real. Yes they missed a golden opportunity by not accepting the king.

Sometimes we get the wrong information that is informed by Satan people.

43

Chapter IX

David
David Sons

Ammon- Ahinoam the Jezreelitess

Daniel/Chileab-Abigal the Carmelitess

Absalom-Maacah & Sister Tamar.

Adonijah-Haggith

Shephatiah-Abital

Ithream-Eglah =These six sons were born in Hebron

Shimea-Bath-Sheba   "

44

Shobab-Bath-Sheba "

Solomon-Bath-Sheba born in Jerusalem

Other sons by David wives or concubines.

Ibhar

Elishua/Elishama-

Nogah

Eliphelet

Nepheg

45

Japhia

Elishama

Eliada-Beeliada

Eliphelet

Jerimoth

46

David and Bethsheba

David & Bath-sheba sons

01. Solomon

02. Shimea

03. Shobab-

04. Nathan

05. Nogah

47

Chapter X

Solomon

The last born in David's old age. His colored skin with bushy hair made him stand out and looked like the future Christ.

His elder brother Adonijah tried to wrestle the crown away. David knew Solomon would be the best choice to be King.

48

Chapter XI

Jesus Christ

Jesus Christ was not a Jew. Christ was a Nazirite. A Nazirite was abstain from wine, strong or intoxicating drinks.

He also had a skin color, therefore when he got older traveling in the sun his feet look like burnt brass and hair like lamb wool.

Most westerners describe him as fair skin with straight hair. This is far out fiction.

49

Chapter XII

Who are God's Children?

"We all are God's children". This is something I heard from a little boy. Now I am a man and I have found out that is not true.

God's children exhibit justice and righteousness.

He selected a family from Jacob's seed to produce an ideal people to make him happy.

This did not work to well. Jacob had twelve (12) sons of which were promised a family of Israelites. In the beginning things went fairly well. Things later began to tumble when some families thought they were better than the others.

Let us see what happen. Jacob and Leah had their first son Reuben. Then they had Simeon their second son. A third son named Levi. A fourth son name Judah. Now these sons with light skin call themselves full brothers.

Jacob now went and had a fifth son Dan by Leah's maid Bilhah. This son had colored skin. He had a sixth son Naphtali by Bilhah. This son also had colored skin. Now these two sons are full brothers.

A seventh son came name Gad by Rachel's maid Zilpah. This son has colored skin. An eighth son came by Zilpah name Asher which he had colored skin also. These two sons are full brothers to each other.

51

Jacob went back to Leah and had a ninth son named Issachar. He also had another son with Leah and named him Zebulun. This makes six sons he had with Leah all light skinned.

Jacob and Rachel had a son and called him Benjamin. They had another son and called him Joseph. These two sons are full brothers.

We learned how people treat or act differently toward people with different skin types. We assume the six children by Leah are the same.

We also know that the two from Bilhah are Canaanites. They are from the bloodline of Ham. They have a skin color.

52

We believe that Zilpah sons have a skin color.

We were taught that Laban daughter Rachel was fare skinned.

Her two sons could fit in but were they?

All twelve sons of Jacob suppose to be the Israelites. Now where are Bilhah and Zilpah children? Are they supposed to be part of this Godly family? Where are they? Are they excluded because of their skin color?

We do know that everywhere and anywhere the Israelites traveled Dan and Naphtali families were always behind. They never travel in front or middle of the group.

53

Many scholars would try to offer an explanation to not show racism within the pack. Just like in America, laws are made to to satisfy a certain nation.

Never-the-less it cannot be denied because this same action spilled over in the western world.

Here we are in a world with different nations. How many of these nations preach peace to the other nations?

I will let you answer that question by saying children of God would preach peace instead of firing weapons at their enemy throwing rocks.

54

If you think this is the proper actions of God children then Satan has you all wrapped up. How do I know this?

I know this by ways and actions of our laws and how they are carried out. You will do things unlawful and change laws that against God's law. Your popularity means more than exercising righteous actions that pleasing to God.

Some of the children of Jacob want to hold on to being God's children. I do understand because this gives them privileges to do ungodly things and get by. You want the world to see you as God's children and support all your acts.

55

The Jewish nations miss a great golden opportunity by denying and not accepting Jesus Christ as their King.

Jesus Christ came to fulfill his Father's prophecy for the Jewish nation. When the Jews denied him this spilled over to the Gentiles.

The Pharisees and Sadducees wanted to hold on to Moses's law and not accept the fulfillment if God's law.

He sent his disciples to teach all nations and baptize them in the name of the Father, Son and the Holy Ghost.

When Jesus died on the cross; he died for everyone, and if you believe in him you will be saved. That every living soul. No one excluded in this path through Jesus Christ.

Many didn't believe in Jesus Christ because he had a skin color. It was easy for the Jews to yell "Kill him!"

I have listen to the television Evangelists and most of the older ministries teach from the Old Testament. I seldom hear them mention Jesus Christ. I do understand too.

You are trying to hold on to a worldly phrase that going to send you to hell.

57

When you enter this worldly phase door it will lead you thru a tunnel.

Traveling thru this tunnel you will meet all kinds of sins. These ungodly sins the Devil will try to make you believe it alright to try once. That is all he needs for you to do is try it once.

This power of Satan will have you sinning over and over again.

Therefore it's very important that you defeat Satan.

No one! I mean no one get to the Kingdom of God unless you are borne again. When you are borne again Christians will know. All God's children are born again.

58

Chapter XIII

What is really borne again?

We all join a church and are baptized. We are not born just in this act. We have to grow and become strong in the power of God.

Man is borne in a world of sin. Jesus died on the cross and shed his blood which paid the penalty for our sins. This gives us the chance of redemption and takes our lives back from Satan.

Once you learn about the strength of God fear sets in. Your old body will die. When your old body dies and the new body takes over then you give your life completely to God. Then and only then you will be borne again. Why do I be strong about this?

59

I am strong about this because to be borne again means you have to become a new person. Your old body has died. You are regenerated by the Holy Spirit and you take on a new body. This is the only way to get into God's Kingdom.

How this can happen? Your body must die and a new body emerges from the one that dies. Now you have a new body. That old sinful body is gone and you have a new one.

Let me give you an example: When you plant a cornel of corn in the ground; this corn dies and bring forth new corn. This is the way a body must make the same change.

Another good example is when Jesus Christ died on the cross. When he was raised from the dead he had the doors of Heaven open to him. When you are borne again the door of Heaven will open for you.

Let me point out you cannot be borne again today and tonight you go out clubbing. Do not let anyone fool you about the ins and outs. When you are borne again you are solid in God's faith.

We had Ministers who audience filled a football stadium. When he come to a question where to go against his nationality, countryman or a different race he paused or will not give a direct answer.

61

You have the police killing unarmed African Americans and not one will rise up and say this is wrong. They want say that because they will lose their clout with friends and neighbors. They only say we need Jesus.

We had one well known Minister to go on television and say 'When the police tell you to stop he means stop" What he is saying if this young scared boy runs its ok for the police to shoot him in the back.

This comes from one of those Ministers that fill football fields. A child of God hears this they don't have to say anything, but they will know this man is not saved. He is after money and fame.

62

When this happen everyone who is born again knows this is a hypocrite and just out to make money, easy job and a big name for him.

We have many ministers in this country that recognizes the ugly conflicts of police killing unarmed men. No one have come out and said anything against this violence.

Why they have not spoken out? They are unsaved and not borne again. They know if they speak out most of their family, friends and neighbors will judge against him.

A new body borne with God's DNA provides the knowledge and power God meant for men to have on this earth.

63

We use this word many times in today's world; DNA. When you become a child of God you have his DNA. What? Are you kidding me? This is very simple if I have a child, that child has my DNA.

If you become a child of God you must have his DNA. That is the reason of being borne again. Your body has changed from sin to righteousness.

The only way you can defeat Satan is becoming a child of God. With God's DNA your soul is absolutely free from worldly sins.

With God's DNA your body takes on cells and characteristics (heredity) of Jesus Christ. This body then becomes an heir to God's Kingdom. You are now born again and become a child of God.

Therefore you cannot change back into that sinful world. Fear keeps you from making mistakes.

The experts will examine this book and try to make everything wrong. They will make you think you can go out and party, do all those sinful things and come back to him in the morning.

They want to stay in control of your life. They do not want you to resist their way of life. They makes the laws, break them and when they get to court, the Judge find them innocence. There is no win for you.

Now when this person is speaking, please examine him closely. You will be looking in the eyes of Satan.

65

Ask yourself "why is he doing this?" "Is there something he does not want me to know?' He will try to put your life on a different trail.

Many people have to separate themselves from friends and family in order to serve God righteously.

God bless the righteousness and those that have the ability to do things pleasing to him.

Those who seek God's Kingdom must travel down a narrow road. This narrow road is not going to church saying a prayer and your work is done. There is work down this narrow road you must do.

At the end of your narrow road you will not have any earthly treasured. All your treasures will be in heaven.

66

Most of us work all our lives to be a millionaire. This is what sends people to hell.

We steal, lie and take people property to become millionaires.

Eighty-five (85%) per cent of our millionaires are robbers and thieves. They rob the poor and sell their goods rocket high to make unfair profits. Let me give you an example.

A farmer plants corn. In order for that farmer to make a good living for him and his family; he must sale his corn for a dollar an ear. Let's say the value of this ear of corn is three dollars.

67

Here comes a buyer for his corn. The buyer knows the value of this corn is three dollars an ear. What the buyer does is try to buy this farmer corn for less than a dollar.

When this happens the farmer and his family lose money by a selfish and greedy buyer who wants to make a lot of money.

Eventually this buyer will become a millionaire and the people will worship his avenues to richness. They all are going to hell.

Take a look around you. The millionaires and billionaires want you to look up to them. They all have built up treasures here on earth, to die and go to hell leaving all there treasures behind.

68

Do not let anyone fool you; you cannot be a monster all you life and instantly go to God's Kingdom. God must see favor in you to open his Kingdom gate.

Jesus is standing at the gate. You got to go thru Jesus to get to God's Kingdom.

Let me tell you this; when you look up and realize a veil is not over your eyes, you are headed for God's Kingdom. There is no darkness in your life and you see the world in a difference way.

You will meet Satan and recognize him. That is the reason for this false preaching. Satan wants to stay hidden behind false preaching. He wants to control your mind.

69

Get on the trail of this narrow road to God's Kingdom and light will shine on you forever.

I meet many people who disagree with my thoughts. I do understand, they want to have room in their life to do what they want to and not God.

They want to continue to go out and play and ask God to forgive them at the end. This is many of ways people lives and expect you to believe they are saved.

This is not the way and life of a child of God. A child of God is vigilant at all times. He constantly trying to get people to change their way of life because he knows they are going to hell.

Why is he vigilant? When you become a child of God, you love everybody and want the best for people who are not borne again.

As I walk the streets I meet people who turn their head and look the other way when passing.

I pray for them because I know they have a problem.

Again when I meet someone with smiles and greet me with a godly greeting; that bring a smile upon my face.

God's people are not dumb just because they listen to your speech. They know when you are lying to them. God give them knowledge to know when a false statement is made.

71

All God children are happy people. Why are they happy? When you know you are borne again; that happiness exceeds any happiness man can have on this earth.

Let me tell you a true story which you should have read about.

This lady had a pain in her chest. She went to the Doctor and had an x-ray performed. This x-ray shows a spot on her lung. The Doctor said an operation was required for removal.

Her husband and family members all were with her having this operation.

When she went in the hospital for this operation she had a troubled mine of dissatisfaction.

72

After being prep for the operation she asked for another x-ray because she knew her body was the body of Christ and Christ never fail her.

Another x-ray was performed and the spot was gone. The Doctor and technicians could not understand what happen. The lady in question understood because she knew all them do not have the power of God.

This story wasn't run much because certain people do not want you to believe what the power of God can do you.

If you are borne again you are a child of God. The gates of Heaven are open for you. God reveal many mysteries to his children. Are you borne again? Are you a child of God?

73

Chapter XIV

Racism and the Bible

The Western world has rewritten the Bible scripts as European people. They have created a scene that all bible characters are European people.

People in the east know this is not true and call the westerners Satan and liars. People in the west claims they know more about the east than the people who have live there all their life.

Please we so not give people credit. Common sense tells everybody no other country can tell you more about your country than you who lived there all your life. This is racism.

Numbers 12:1-10 tells how God disapprove of Racism. Leprous was what God laid on Moses Sister for her actions against his color skin wife from Ethiopia..

Thank about the Racism in the world today. It's so common that it is hard to recognize. This has become a way of life and most westerners believe this is the way to live.

What went on years ago is still going on today. Many people who are affected by this and try to ignore it existence is guilty as well. This is a terrible situation to try to live with. This is a continuing act by Satan people. (Not God's people).

75

I have to include this short message: I was just watching television when a Judge beat-up his wife. Would you believe they plan to do nothing?

A few weeks ago an African American football player slapped his wife because she spit on him and he had the book thrown at him. Do you see how unfair this country is?

Our Judges are off the chain. They do whatever makes their friends happy. A boned again man knows a Judge should judge for God and not man. Racism is the results of his judgment.

God knows not too much good can be in store for any country that practice racism.. This is not going to change; this way of life for Japheth descendents are built in.

76

Satan has a plan set for all people to become leaders. Let us talk about the United States. This is a country that God has blessed. If you become the President and try to help poor people; you stand a chance of getting assassinated. Why?

Would a Godly country assassinate his head? Look at our Judges. Are they guided by the laws of God or the laws of man? Most of our Judges are guided by the laws made by man. There is nothing Godly about these laws.

We have forgotten what happen in the real bible days. The people that lived in the East all their lives have full knowledge of what happen in their World. We in the West want to manage other nation's activities.

77

I refused to mention some of our activities. They are so unpleasant to think about much less to see.

Never-the-less we have great people in all nations. This is the reason we as people must love all nations. Not just because of a skin color but because of who we are and what we want to be.

We cannot classify us as children of God with all this hate built inside of us. Satan have got many of us fooled that we have the righteous way to go. We make our own truth and paths.

He places his lawmakers in the right place to pass certain laws.

He places certain Police Officers in positions to make us uncomfortable. Within no time his plans work. The Godly people voices are left out and they inherit punishments.

Remember Jacob's children Dan, Naphtali, Gad and Asher. These children have colored skin. Every where the Israelites traveled these children had to travel in the back behind the pack.

<u>Dan the fifth son of Jacob had the second highest number of people but received the smallest amount of territory when the promise land was divided. That is totally ashamed.</u> **<u>You know this displeases God.</u>**

79

There you see how ungodly people were yesterday and how ungodly they are today. The same situation is use in many ways to keep you from recognizing that they are Satan.

Dan had colored skin and this is what ungodly people do. But I will assure you one day; one day will come when all these sins will be paid. You must believe me this is not going to be good.

Why did Dan receive so little when he had such large tribe? His tribe was dark skin people. This is so sad when the Israel's suppose to be Godly people.

The other which has fair skin closed ranks within Jacob's other children. They want the World to believe they are the only ones as the Children of Israel.

They wanted to keep this a secret but the East knows this and only Satan people would do such a thing..

(This was added after the first publication). The Prime Minister from that New State of Israel came to the United States and would not speak or recognize our President Obama because he is black, This is a racist nation).

We as a people must believe sooner or later the truth will come out and set you free.

Ancient Assyrian-Babylonian area of NE Africa known as the "Middle East" was Inhabited by the Hamitic & Shemitic. They had No problems living side by side.

Japheth bloodline could not live in peace besides the families of Shem or Ham.

81

Could that be the reason why God only gave Japheth fourteen nations? God gave Shem twenty-six nations and Ham thirty nations.

Watch and listen what the experts say about that. Believe me they will come up with some sort of answer. When they bring forth their answer please take a long look at Satan. That right!!! You see Satan in the flesh.

Come now folks open your eyes and stop believing all that propaganda. Search for the truth and you will find it.

It is a shame that all nations cannot sit and speak with each other. There isn't one nation who is perfect. All nations have flaws and misunderstanding values.

Therefore there is no one nation should rule over another. All nations' heads should come together and resolve their differences with each nation equal a single vote.

Racism or any person with a racism background should not be allowed to attend these meetings.

Tell me a country where there are colored skin people and no racism exists.

Horrible isn't it?

83

Chapter XV

How we should live?

We as a people want to escape our responsibility as a parent and teacher of our children. It is the parent duty to live a true life and teach their children and grandchildren to do the same.

If a parent lives a true life he can expect his grandchildren to be successful. I want you to know every ugly thing that a parent does bring ugliness to his grandchildren. In every word I am saying God will bless your grandchildren if you live a Godly life.

See children with ugly diseases, body deformed and very troublesome. Look back at their family history and you will see the cause.

84

Many try to ignore their grandfather habits or conditions.

This also applies to jobs, states and countries.

If a job treats his employees unfairly, this job will soon fall. If states make laws to cause their people to suffer, soon this state will suffer some form of punishment. Never-the-less we cannot forget about a country.

Countries hold a big assert in the treatment of his people. Dictatorship is one of the worst things that can happen to a country. Some Dictators respect their people and things usually work well. The people are paid well and wealth is divided equally.

85

Slavery is number one in any country. It would not be terrible if the people were given respect. It when you live in a condition of fear. Not knowing if someone going to kick your door down and hang you for nothing.

Living this type of life is beyond reproach. I am sure their blood cry out to the Lord and someday, in some way, someone will pay the price for this action.

Many will say I had nothing to do with that back in the day. Tell that to God and he will tell you your forefathers cause the suffering he is going to receive.

Everything goes back to where the incidents happen. There is no escape. Everyone must pay for their wrong doing.

86

Therefore we must ask ourselves; do we want our grandchildren to suffer? Do we want our great grandchildren to suffer? If we do not we must live a Godly life to insure our children have a great future.

Let me tell you this story. Six young kids some fifty years ago going to college got caught smoking pot. He and his friends went to court. Some of his friends got probation but two of them got charged with a felon.

Why were two given a felon when all doing the same thing? Do I have to tell you!!! Two of these boys were African AMERICANS.

I spoke with one of these men after someone broke into his house. He was very glad he wasn't at home because he probably would be killed. I asked him if he was at home he could have stopped them with his gun. Then he told me; he applied for a gun for his home and they said he could not get one because he was a felon some fifty years ago.

I had to think for a few minutes. Then I thought who in their right mind would make a law for a nonviolence felon record to last fifty years?

This is an outrage and a shame. Our lawmakers do not have the knowledge because they do seek God for answers. They think they are above everybody but they are the lowest.

A nonviolent felon should last no longer than two years and no more than three years at the most. Why did not the Judge charge all with the same sentence? Does he know there should be equal justice? This is another reason we need Judges who judge for God and not man.

This is why we need lawmakers that know Christ.

Lawmakers who entrust their thoughts to God will always make the right decision. What kind of lawmakers we have now? You guess it. I cannot write it because it's too ugly.

89

May 11, 2014 I happen to turn on my television and Pastor Charles Stanley was speaking.

He said one phrase that every living person should do. "Listen to God". This sums everything up in a person's life. Listen to God!!!

If we listen to God many of our problems would be solved. This should hit our Judges and lawmakers hard. Most Judges and lawmakers listen to their acquaintances for answers.

Out of all your Harvard's degrees there is nothing can match a degree from God's Kingdom? Harvard degrees make you think you are perfect and better equip to make decisions.

This idea has destroyed many people and nations and eventually will destroy your world unless you listen to God.

Great leaders listen to God. You cannot become a great leader without leadership and knowledge of God. Great leaders rule on the knowledge of God which exhibits righteousness and justice.

Great leaders have many enemies. This world is filled with sinful people and a righteous leader would not fit into their schedule.

Ungodly leaders Practices and disobey God's rules and this development becomes a non-believing nation. They desire richness and lust to benefit their cause for living.

91

Richness is what drives most people to sin. Eighty-five (85%) per cent of our millionaires are robbers and thieves. They rob the poor and sell their goods rocket high to make unfair profits.

Many nations had the idea that a rich nation was in God's favor.
God know that richness is where a man heart is. Therefore, if you store your treasures in heaven this will please God.

We must take care of our poor people. They must be treated with respect and kindness. God command this from his children.

We should love one another and not hate our brothers and sisters.

92

Just to help you understand the meaning of hatred; I picked up an old magazine to read because of it title.

When I read the title "The Antichrist" and look at the cover I did not open this magazine. This Magazine had our President on the cover. That automatically told me who the antichrist is. How can anyone posses so much hate.

Let me add something very special. We should get rid of all images.
All those pictures on your wall of Jesus Christ will send you to Hell. That is one reason the people in the East are not afraid of the people in the West. They know we are praying to images and that is not the way God outlined our way of living.

93

They call the people in the West Devils and Satan. Why? Because they know all about what happen in their country. They know Jesus Christ did not come through the bloodline of Japheth.

It's quite understandable; when you read Japheth bloodline from Noah you will find there is no contribution of any good thing written. Never-the-less he takes on the names of Ham and Shem bloodline, in books and movies to make the world think his bloodline played a part.

This action create an unwanted among people living in the East who know Jesus Christ and where he came from. Many will say it only a movie.

Then one brother told me the West would not like an African American playing George Washington in a movie. I had to accept his subjection because it is the truth.

Another ugly living condition is the way we dress. Women especially wear short clothing to make her appeal beautiful before men. That is one common thing that most people do not talk about and it ungodly.

If she only knew that dressing that way tell the world that she is a worldly woman, a slut and her mind is fruitless. A saved man would not under any condition consider her as a partner. An intelligent woman neither would nor expose her body to the world.

95

A woman looks beautifully when she wears a dress at least to her knees. If she wears pants they are not the skin tight women wear today. Why we don't have ministers preaching this to the people?

Another move is when a woman gets on television she sits and cross her legs with a short dress leaving the cameras room to look at her upper leg. That tells the world that she is no good.

This might be good ratings for the television station because their rating will go up. Sinful people love to look at sinful things. More and more we are leaving our children to learn ungodly living.

96

When we go to the beach to have a cook out and enjoy the sun. We see women with almost nothing on. Do you think God is please with that? No and you will not say anything because you are not saved. A person saved will look at that in a disgusting manner.

We cry freedom but freedom to do ungodly things should be reversed.
Yes it should be ungodly for women or men to go out almost necked.

There is a television preacher who I loved to watch. He and his wife is a beautiful couple. He has a large church and ministering a few years. One Sunday as I began to watch I was shocked. His wife came on stage wearing a short dress. She always has dressed decent and nicely. I guess Satan walked thru their door. I never watched his program again.

97

I look at nations who dressing in a godly manner. These nations do not have many humanity violations. You will find there is God among them.

God nations have a Godly friendship around the world.

Their ladies are fully dressed (not showing their under panties) and their men love all nationalities. They know the last days are here.

We as a nation should have an obligation to God to fulfill our duties according to God's law. This insured us and gives us security in our thinking, duties and goals. This is the greatest protection we can have.

98

2 Timothy 3: 1-4 & 17 reads: 1.This know also, that in the last days perilous times shall come.

For many shall be lovers of their own selves, covetous, boasters, proud, blasphemers, disobedient to parents, unthankful, unholy,.

Without natural affection, trucebreakers, false accusers, incontinent, fierce, despisers of those that are good.

We have traitors, high-minded, lovers of pleasures more than lovers of God.

Idolatry, drunkenness, Prostitution, tattooing the flesh and favoritism is not a favorite activity of God's plan.

99

Look around you; how many family, friends or neighbors fit in this category?

That the man of God may be perfect, thoroughly furnished unto all good worked.

One thing I would like to mention. Man has put himself above God. When God said "Thou shall not kill"; this is a statement from him which is not debatable. Man cannot debate God's word.

We have let Satan make complete fools of ourselves. We have let Satan into our lives and have destroyed many other lives.

Satan has got it going on. He teaches the teacher and the teacher teaches us.

100

Chapter XVI

Noted Bible Women

Aalif

An Arabian Ethiopian lived in Midian, A country established by Hamites

Delilah-Samson's downfall

Dinah-Jacob's daughter

Hagar-

Hagar=an Egyptian slave girl. Mother of Ishmael

101

Jezebel- As a queen Influence many with her fornications and sorceries.

Queen Candance- Queen Candace+ (Acts 8:27) Ethiopian Queen

Queen of Sheba

Queen of Sheba was from today called Yemen

Queen of Sheba-Was from that part of Ethiopia occupied by two grandsons of Cush. (Sheba and Dedan) She had a son with Solomon and called him Menelik. She was also known as Queen of the South.

102

Zipporah-Moses's Wife

God put leprosy on Moses sister Miriam because she discriminated against his black wife.

It so horrible all the discrimination in the United States and they want us to honor the flag. The flag supposed to mean justice for all. That is not what is happening in these United States. Everyone would love to say this is the best country in the world but we have racists running this country and that the problem.

103

Things you might want to know.

The African Oyo tribe which is a Yoruba family kidnapped Africans for the slave traders.

The traders were Japheth children Dodanim, Meshech and Tubal.

The slaves were kidnapped and sold to the Portuguese people for guns and horses.

The Portuguese sold the slaves to the western states.

One thing the Oyo tribe did not know was they kidnapped seeds that were from the tribe of Dan.
Dan is one of the dark skin Israelites.

104

You don't know and I will not tell you because you will conflict harm upon them. But I will tell you this they will not marry a foreign wife or husband.

There are five other tribes that you know off. One of them will do anything for lust or money.

The other knows the secret but stay unknown because this country is known for assassinations.

They know one day we got to pay for all the ugliness that we do. That is where Isis gets the idea of cutting a person head off.

Slave Masters done this to run away slaves. They would cut their heads off or hung them in the streets. SAD

105

Absolute

The Devil has made excellent progress in the last hundred years.
His tactics mostly undetectable are design to lead people in his direction.
Today this world is a mess. He used color to separate and information to make him looks Godly.

Let's check some of his successes. He placed men in key positions to make and change laws to his benefit.

What has he done?
1. He placed officials in positions to make new laws of his wishes.

2. He will not let you disciple your child. Your children grow up knowing he or she can do what-ever and the parent cannot legally do a thing.

106

3. He used color to distribute undetectable behavior in division of nations.

4. In placing writings the Holy Bible; he disregarded mostly all Hamitic life and four children of Jacob. Those children are Dan, Naphteli, Gad and Asher.

5. He used mostly the life of Shem which is the bloodline of Jesus Christ. This is a good thing.

6. He placed people in position to use Japheth nation to proclaim they are the good ones in the Holy Bible. How? They change the color of the original (rightful) nation to make the world believe they are the ones written about.

107

7. Once again he used lawmakers to make an ungodly law to unite two males or two females. This law strikes down God's law from the beginning of life. Marriage is the union of one man and one woman. Anything else is satanic.

Man has really gone ungodly. I do not see this world lasting much longer. I am sure God is going to do something about this.

What hurt the most are all our Ministers who teach God's law sits back quietly. Are they afraid to say anything? Are they really true God's teachers? Why don't they say something? If they are afraid they should **SIT DOWN** and **SHUT UP!!!**

108

It is great to see two people married the way God recommended, Man and woman. If a marriage is not consummated under God's law it's a sin. People see ungodly marriage and turn their head. Why is all this happening? Does everyone accept this as true living? Do I hear a voice calling God's children together? Try listening quietly in a dark room; you just might hear a voice calling you.

This nation is doing many ungodly things. God just let us have the rope to hang ourselves. Our lawmakers; they lusts, greed and any ungodly path is sending us into an early ending.

I fear our Heavenly Father is not going to let this go on forever.

109

I want to leave something for Preachers to tell their congregations.

Tell them what nation that gathered up all the books that God's inspired men written; took out what they wanted the world to know then; buried some and the rest hid them in caves. Yes your audience has a right to know, do you know?

Some of these books were discovered in 1948. They are still trying to keep this a secret. This is the ugliest nation in this world. Teachers and Preachers tell the world the truth!!!!!

110

www.ingramcontent.com/pod-product-compliance
Lightning Source LLC
LaVergne TN
LVHW011426080426
835512LV00005B/282